The Magic of Bangkok

CONTENTS

Great City of Angels

The people of Thailand know their capital city as Krungthep – City of Angels – a short form of the official Thai name that stretches to over 40 letters and which roughly translates as follows: Great city of angels, supreme repository of divine jewels, great unconquerable land, grand and renowned realm, royal and enchanting capital city, home of the nine noble gems, highest royal domicile and grand palace, holy shelter and abode of the reincarnated spirits.

The name Bangkok, which comes from the Thai term for the original site where king Rama I ordered the building of a new city in the 1780s, stuck with foreigners as it was much easier to pronounce, and so the city took on its dual designation.

This duality offers a useful way of getting to the heart of Bangkok's identity and its ability to astonish visitors, whether they come from a foreign country or from a rural province of

Above Bangkok's Buddhist monks do not secrete themselves away behind the walls of monasteries; they are part of the everyday human landscape of the metropolis.

Left The prayer-like gesture of the traditional Thai greeting – the wai – is used as a general greeting and farewell and as a mark of acknowledgement.

Thailand itself. For while Bangkok looks like a quintessentially Asian metropolis – chaotic, ad hoc, Third Worldish in places – the city is also hedonistically Western, consumer-driven, and seemingly dedicated to excess. This hybrid of East and West extends beyond skyscrapers and shopping malls: Bangkok is no Singapore or Kuala Lumpur, and whatever resemblance it shares with those two cities is merely skin deep. The fusion of cultures and lifestyles that drives Bangkok is far from being superficial, but what it is exactly that makes Bangkok a world city is hard to fathom. It is not multicultural in the manner of London or New York, though there are Chinese and Indian communities, and the constant influx of a wide variety of foreign visitors, staying for days, months and years, is part of its appeal.

Above View across the city from the Landmark Hotel – a modest number of high-rise buildings characterize the typical Bangkok skyline in the centre of the city.

Familiar media images of the city, from temples to strip clubs, are like travel cliches everywhere which tend to disguise as much as they reveal. To say that Bangkok is a mass of contradictions hardly helps the understanding of its unique heartbeat, though it is difficult to know how else one can come to terms with its central dichotomy. For somehow, coexisting with the neon and the traffic and the debilitating heat, Bangkok is a city of enviable poise and refinement. Accepting what seems like chaos and sensing the dignity with which people go about their ordinary lives – this is the magic of Bangkok.

Above Containing holy relics of the Buddha, this temple tower is known as a prang and its distinctive appearance bears the influence of Khmer art forms.

History of Bangkok

Some ten million people – around one in eight of the national population – live, work and sleep in an area formed by alluvial deposits from the Chao Phraya River that flows from the north into the Gulf of Thailand. Years ago, as the mudbanks solidified, families of fishing folk built dwellings on stilts and gradually farmers moved in to plant rice in the rich alluvial soil that had formed. Bangkok's metamorphosis from mudswamp to megacity took place over a millennium, starting around 500AD when the mudbanks first began to rise above sea level. It was not long before the community developed to such a size that the local king began to take notice.

Above One of the classic postures of Buddha statues, with the right hand resting on the plinth or the ground, signifies an episode in Buddha's life when he touched the earth as a witness to his strength of mind.

Around 1500AD, an independent Thai kingdom had been in existence for nearly three centuries. Based in the north of the country, first at Sukhothai and then annexing territory further to the north, the first Thai kingdom had gradually spread its influence southwards. By the beginning of the 16th century, the centre of Thai power had shifted irreversibly to the south at Ayutthaya, on the Chao Phraya River, and a powerful, centralized, monarch-based state had emerged. There followed a golden age of Thai prosperity, with Dutch and then French traders gaining royal favours, marred only by power struggles within the monarchy and the gradual re-emergence of an old enemy, the Burmese. In 1767, the Burmese successfully lay siege to Ayutthaya and four centuries of Thai civilization went up in smoke. It did not take long for an enterprising Thai soldier to fill the power vacuum created by the vanquished Thai royalty and the Burmese were quickly repelled. The new leader, Taksin, took stock of the situation and decided Ayutthaya was not worth rebuilding when a new capital could be

Above Rama I brought bricks downriver from the ancient capital of Ayutthaya to build the wall for the new city of Bangkok and the Grand Palace.

more securely situated closer to the sea. The village of what is today known as Bangkok seemed a suitable location. It was close to the sea but still on the Chao Phraya River, and Taksin chose the west bank of the river for his base. He became the new king of Siam, as the country was known up until 1939, and by the time he died, Bangkok was definitely on the map.

Deposed in a power struggle, the fate of Bangkok's first military leader, Taksin, was to be echoed in later centuries by many other generals. In 1782 a new general, named Chakri, took over and instituted a new royal line and a dynasty that still reigns today. General Chakri, also known as Rama 1, set about creating a city worthy of his ambitious plans for Thai hegemony. He moved across the Chao Phraya River to its east bank and the Chinese traders already there shifted to the southeast to what is today Bangkok's Chinatown. Canals were dug for transport, city walls erected and a palace built before Rama I died at the beginning of the 19th century. Rama II and Rama III continued their predecessor's efforts of creating a capital fit for a king and

Above This highly ornate guardian figure is one of several that surround a golden chedi in the grounds of the Grand Palace.

5

reopened Siam to foreign influences. But the king who would leave the biggest mark on Bangkok was Rama IV, who ascended to the throne in 1851.

Poetic license taken by Hollywood filmmakers often presents little more than a semblance of reality – this may help account for Yul Brynner's inaccurate portrayal of Rama IV in the 1956 film, The King and I. Perhaps it suited the West to imagine Asian rulers as inept and frivolous, but Rama IV and his son achieved plenty to deconstruct this image. King Mongkut, as Rama IV became known, opened his country to the West without allowing it to become just another colony for Britain or France. The process was creatively continued by his son and by the dawn of the 20th century Bangkok could boast an electric tram system and other benefits of modern technology. It is notable indeed that Siam's development and modernization took place without foreign domination, even though Britain and France colonized and exploited all her neighbours.

The era of absolute rule by a king came to an end in the 1930s when a palace coup ushered in a new constitutional monarchy. In the decades after World War II, Bangkok was the epicentre of a series of military coups, failed constitutional governments and widespread corruption fostered by US aid during the Cold War and the Vietnam War. In retrospect, the catastrophic economic crisis that occurred in 1997 can be seen as the inevitable consequence of the unchecked, fast-money mentality that had characterized Bangkok's

Above King Bhumibol Adulyadej of Thailand – the name translates as Strength of the Land, Incomparable Power – has a role in Thai society out of all proportion to his formal standing.

identity for too long. The city's nemesis took the form of IMF-dictated counter-measures that put thousands out of work and saw businesses and financial institutions collapse like dominos. Only in the last couple of years have the citizens of Bangkok emerged from the trauma of the economic crisis produced by decades of rampant capitalism.

Right Vimanmek Palace in Dusit Park, constructed by Rama V in 1901, is the largest golden teakwood mansion in the world.

Culture and Religion

Western expressions like 'being cool' and 'chilling out' refer more to a mannered pose – a way one would like to be or be seen – than any deep-rooted calmness of mind. In Bangkok the reverse is true: there is a sense of placidity amidst the hubbub. Tell this to most Thais who live in small towns away from the capital and they would probably disagree – to them, life in the megacity is frenzied and decidedly 'uncool'. New visitors arriving by plane or train will tend to agree, but this is only because international airports and train stations are chaotic anyway. It will take a chance occurrence or, ideally, an opportunity to share a social occasion with city dwellers in order to sense the quality of *sanuk* (good fun)

Above The ubiquitous three-wheeled taxi of Bangkok, the *tuk-tuk*, gets its name from the characteristic sound of its small but noisy engine.

which lies at the heart of the Thai character. A cynic once summed up this basic quality as the ability to work at play and play at work, but it is not really such a lightweight philosophy. It is, instead, an essential part of Bangkok's appeal and the beauty that emerges from the concrete jungle.

Business and commerce are tackled in Bangkok in pretty much the same way they would be in most capital cities of the world, but the quality of *sanuk* is always evident in the background. Just

as the city itself is a strange hybrid of East and West, the citizens too reveal an enviable ability to balance the demands of work and play. Bangkok's traffic jams are notorious – though no longer spectacularly different to many other megacities of the world – yet it is rare to encounter an incipient brawl between irate drivers. Traffic delays that would seem to test the patience and endurance of most sane people are negotiated with enviable equanimity.

Left Thai visitors to the Grand Palace come to worship as much as they do to gaze at the beautiful buildings around them.

7

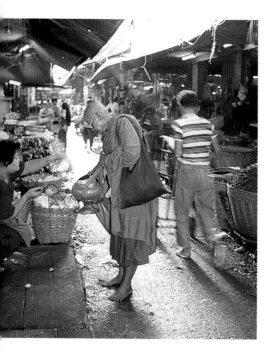

Buddhism has a lot to do with the disarming peace of mind that is still evident in this heaving metropolis, though you can hardly expect shining examples of this state of mind in touristy areas. It helps to acknowledge the fact that Buddhism is more of a philosophy than a religion. After all, Buddhism does not subscribe to a god. It recognizes the incessant and demanding nature of human desire and strives to satisfy it with the yearning for self-knowledge and spiritual contentment. The simple truth that material possessions do not entail happiness is accorded importance and time is always found for spiritual relaxation and the search for everyday enlightenment. A good example of this is to be found at the Erawan Shrine in the heart of the city. The open-air shrine is situated, quite literally, on the corner of two of Bangkok's busiest streets, next to a five-star hotel and adjacent to the huge World Trade Centre, a vulgar shrine in its own way to consumer spending. The Erawan Shrine was originally built as a good-luck gesture when an earlier hotel was first being constructed on the site and a number of mishaps occurred. Nowadays, the shrine is never empty as shoppers and office-workers drop by to make an offering of flowers to the statue of the four-headed Hindu deity or pay a small amount of baht to the dancers and musicians who are often on call for such requests. A steady stream of supplicants fills the small space of the shrine, oblivious to the roar of nearby traffic and intrusive tourists with video cameras.

Above Some 95 per cent of Thai citizens are Buddhists and a monk's life is strictly governed by a series of over 200 rules, including the renunciation of all personal possessions except gifts.

Rise early in the morning and it is not uncommon to see a saffron-robed monk serenely making his way down a side-street with an alms bowl. It would be a fundamental mistake to imagine that this is a form of begging; the monk receives only a handful of rice or other food and those who fill his bowl are pleased to make a contribution. This is Buddhism in practice, a blend of humility and good neighbourliness that has existed for centuries. Not that everyone in Bangkok is a Buddhist: for Muslims, Sikhs, Hindus, and Christians all make their presence and their beliefs felt. Unlike some religions, Buddhism is very much about tolerance and Bangkok, a cosmopolitan city in its own right, absorbs communities of all persuasions.

Right The Erawan Shrine stands in stark contrast to the city's new overhead light railway system, the Skytrain, mounted on huge concrete pillars in the background.

Palaces and Places

The tendency for guidebooks and travel books to splash out with superlatives when describing noted buildings makes it difficult to communicate in words the tangible impact of walking around the Grand Palace in Bangkok. To speak of its dazzling shimmer and its resplendent excess of gold can only hint at the shock effect experienced by the first-time visitor when stepping through the huge double gate set into the castellated walls that surround the palace. Part of its magic is due to the sheer accumulation of two centuries of Thai architectural and decorative styles concentrated densely in one palace complex. Until the era of absolute monarchy came to an end in the early 1930s, the Grand Palace had been the residence of royalty as well as the religious centre of the kingdom since 1782. Different kings were influenced by different styles – Western and Chinese as well as Thai – and each monarch left his stamp in the form of new buildings and new refinements. The combined effect is overwhelming, a visual treat that is hard to equal in any other building complex in the world.

The Grand Palace is a myriad of structures: buildings within buildings composed of shrines, small gardens, giant stucco figures, throne halls and residential palaces. Glittering gold seems to drip off the pediments, multi-coloured porcelain tiles dazzle the eyes and glass mosaics create elaborate and beguiling patterns. The Temple of the Emerald Buddha, surrounded by cloisters, is a feast of pure Thai architecture – an appropriate abode for the occult Emerald Buddha.

Above The formidable Reclining Buddha, Wat Po, is the largest in Thailand. It is 46m (150ft) long, 15m (50ft) high and covered entirely in gold leaf.

Above The forbidding form of the demon guards at the Grand Palace, like the one shown here, are taken from the Hindu epic, the *Ramayana*.

The image was brought to Chiang Rai, in the far north of the country, in the 15th century from India via Ceylon and then abducted to Laos until General Taksin returned it to Siam in the 18th century. The Emerald Buddha, only 66cm (26in) high and 48cm (19in) wide, has three sets of robes which are solemnly changed by the king himself at the start of each season. The scale of holy objects changes dramatically at the nearby Wat Po, Temple of the Reclining Buddha, where the giant reclining figure measures 46m (150ft) long and 15m (50ft) high. Covered in gold leaf, the soles of the Buddha's feet are inlaid with mother-of-pearl designs.

The Grand Palace is a rarefied place but it is only a short walk from the palace to a more plebian aspect of the city that holds its own attractions. This is Banglamphu, defined by its famous Khao San Road, home to backpackers and budget travellers and awash with pavement stalls selling counterfeit goods of all types, from ID cards to designer-wear clothes. This is as much part of Bangkok as the Grand Palace and so too is Patpong, an area famous for its red-light bars and clubs and, incidentally, street stalls that retail a far higher quality of counterfeit goods than anything found along Khao San Road. Patpong was made famous by the arrival of American soldiers on leave from the rigors of Vietnam in the early 1970s and it has now developed into a major tourist attraction open every night of the year.

Below Wat Phra Kaeo, The Temple of the Emerald Buddha, was built by King Rama I who is said to have lived in a small makeshift building nearby while the temple was being constructed.

Well over half the citizens of Bangkok have Chinese blood in them and the city's Chinatown is living testimony to the resilience of the culture that sustained the earliest immigrants to Siam. It is a vibrant part of Bangkok, with a character of its own and narrow streets that are also home to the capital's Indian community. Vegetable markets, the shops of bullion merchants, Chinese temples, neon-lit calligraphics and the aroma of rich spices in the air combine to produce a heady atmosphere that seems a million miles away from the super-stylized elegance of the Royal Palace.

Then there is modern Bangkok, a familiar landscape of fancy hotels and glitzy shopping malls that dominates Siam Square, Silom Road and Sukhumvit Road. Even here though, dotted about, are rare architectural and cultural gems such as Jim Thompson's Thai-style house. Thompson was a remarkable American who came to Thailand at the end of World War II and successfully revived the country's silk industry.

Arts and Crafts

One of the most distinctive Thai art forms is the dance-drama, a discipline thought to have evolved from the shadow puppet shows that date back to the 16th century at least. The puppeteers expressed character and narrative by subtle manipulation of their figures and an aesthetic of movement developed over time which paved the way for an independent form of dance-drama. Both shadow puppet performances and dance find inspiration for their drama in the Hindu epic the Ramayana (Ramakien in Thai), a very long adventurous yarn about a struggle between good and evil that Thai youngsters learn at school. The most elevated form of dance-drama is the speechless khon. A sophisticated audience is able to read the highly stylized movements of the dancers who use elaborate costumes and expressionless masks and are accompanied by an unseen orchestra. Rama and Sita, the heroic central characters of the Ramayana, do not wear masks but other characters are recognized by open-mouthed monkey masks or, in the case of the demons, by snarling, implacable masks that denominate their evil nature.

The music that accompanies dance-drama is a synthesis of musical elements from different areas of Southeast Asia, primarily China, India and Cambodia. In the past, classical Thai music was patronized by the monarchy but, with the demise of absolute monarchy, it is proving more difficult to nurture musicians in what is today a highly refined art form. In Bangkok the visitor is just as likely to come across traditional Thai instruments in a far less elevated arena, that of the Thai boxing stadium. Thai boxing may seem no more an art form than the wrestling phenomena of the USA but there is a dramatic element to muay Thai (Thai boxing) that is more ritualistic than commercial. Contestants approach the ring to the accompaniment of a small but shrieking orchestra and each boxer solemnly bows in the direction of his birthplace and then to the four points of the compass. There then follows the ram muay (boxing dance) in which the boxer goes

Above Thai music is highly complex and the notes of the muscial scale bear little resemblance to those of the European scale.

Right The graceful, controlled movements of traditional Thai dancing are thought to derive from shadow puppet performances of the 16th and 17th centuries.

11

through a series of ceremonial movements to the accompaniment of an oboe-like instrument. Music is maintained throughout the actual boxing match, altering its tempo to suit the action in the ring. What takes place in the ring, though, is unlikely to strike the spectator as possessing a spiritual dimension, even though both contestants wear armbands displaying a small image of the Buddha. The physical kicks and blows are all for real and although muay Thai is now governed by strict regulations and a code of conduct, there was a time in the past when serious injuries and even

Above In Thai boxing, any part of the body except the head may be used to strike a blow at an opponent. In this practice bout, a novice boxer learns how to deliver a kicking stroke.

fatalities were not uncommon. In tourist areas like Phuket, Thai boxing events are organized purely for foreign visitors and standards are inevitably diluted as a consequence. In Bangkok, on the other hand, authenticity is guaranteed and Thai fans pour into the stadiums on a regular basis to watch their favourite boxers.

Part of the fascination of Bangkok is the way it acts as a conduit for craft work from every corner of the country. Bangkok is the single largest market for Thai crafts and visitors see – and purchase – more products in the capital than anywhere else in Thailand. Gaysorn Plaza, opposite the World Trade Centre in the heart of the city, would be just another swanky shopping mall were it not for the Thai Craft Museum Shop that occupies two storeys of the building. As well as the rich array of crafts in the shop itself, dotted around it is a series of stalls laden with garments of silk, wood-carvings, hand-woven fabrics, lacquer work, jewellery, ceramics and a host of craft-based items that are crying out to be packed into one's luggage. The range of fabrics, especially cotton and lustrous silk, is eye-catching and, although it is not difficult to find unscrupulous tailors who promise to deliver a suit of hand-made clothes in 24 hours, reliable tailors will insist on at least two fittings and take a few days to produce clothes of quality and excellent value. Some of the best crafts are made by the hill tribes of northern Thailand and their woven shoulder bags are more competi-tively priced in Bangkok than anywhere else.

Right The Thai silk industry was revived in the 1950s; before then it was confined to poorer regions of the country and Thai royalty preferred imported cloths.

Local Cuisine

Nowhere is the spirit of sanuk more hedonistically open to the experience of all than when Bangkok plays host with Thai cuisine. Based on lemon grass, fish sauce, galangal, garlic, coriander and coconut milk, Thai food is guaranteed to assault your taste buds in varying degrees of intensity. The best restaurants, and some of the best pavement food stalls, are in the capital and they serve all budgets except the super-rich. The most lavish and over-the-top feast in any of the most expensive restaurants will still cost far less than a similarly-inspired splurge in London, New York or Singapore.

What helps to make a meal in Bangkok so memorable is the sheer style and panache with which food is prepared and served. As with Japanese cuisine, serving a meal in a beautiful manner is not viewed as a chore; it is integral to the food experience and, because most dishes take an average of only 10 minutes to cook, there is time and talent that can be devoted to the style of presentation. To relate that small, choice dishes are decoratively arranged on the table, or that vegetables are shaped to resemble flowers or a fish, is a severe under-statement. Suffice it to say that you will gaze in awe at the intricacy of what lies before you and wonder how on earth so much care could be put into something so perishable.

Part of the reason why Thai food never tastes as good in other countries is the simple fact that there is no neighbourhood market selling fresh ingredients such as vegetables, fish, poultry, spices, pickles and herbs. The reputation of the very finest restaurants in

Above One aspect of Thailand's unique food culture – intricately carved fruit and vegetables – strikes many visitors as an art form in its own right.

Right Dried fish, like these at Chatuchak market, might not seem a delicacy but little in Thai cuisine is served without a rich variety of condiments and sauces.

Above Lemon grass, chilli, ginger, garlic, galanga root, basil and coriander are just some of the essential herbs and spices used in everyday cooking.

Bangkok often depends on kitchen staff who are up early in the morning sourcing ingredients alongside fellow-citizens looking for their day's lunch. The markets are a world unto themselves: a riot of unrestrained colour with some decidedly acquired smells emanating from small heaps of shrimp paste.

Arrive at a main Bangkok market early in the morning and *tuk-tuks* – a form of motorized rickshaw seen everywhere in the city – are departing with impossibly large bundles of fruit and vegetables. They speed off to smaller markets for local distribution, passing rare snatches of green such as Lumpini Park where early risers, mostly middle-aged, are already jiving to taped pop music for physical exercise. Chinese residents of Bangkok are also here, gracefully executing the centuries-old gestures of tai chi. An hour or so later, on the rooftop of the Grand Hyatt Erawan, executives are pacing around the outdoor jogging track and if they pause to peer down on the street below, they may glimpse a flower-seller arriving at the Erawan Shrine to proffer garlands of

Above Although now somewhat of a tourist attraction, the floating markets in and around Bangkok function in much the same way as they did a century ago.

Above Too many prawns for one diner? Thai dishes are usually served with the intention of being shared by everyone around the table.

Right This vendor at a floating market outside Bangkok will be open for business at 4am and expect to close up shop around three hours later.

jasmine and incense sticks to the first devotees of the morning. Masses of motorcycles, buses, *tuk-tuks* and cars are purring behind red traffic lights at the huge intersection adjacent to the shrine. When the lights change, scores of vehicles simultaneously roar into motion and accelerate as far as the next junction. Another day has begun in the life of Bangkok and breakfast stalls are already busy serving beancurd soup and noodles from oversized woks. Some of the food will have been prepared the night before or earlier that morning. Buddhist monks are out and about to receive their daily offerings of food. Charity and commerce, seemingly odd partners, fuel the souls and stomachs of Bangkok citizens. Late at night, food vendors will be even busier serving up the last meals of the day. As they pack away their mobile kitchens, the bulk of traffic finally subsides but, on the outskirts of the city, huge trucks – many of them so gaily decorated as to be minor works of arts in their own right – are arriving with more food for the next day. There is always activity somewhere in the city for this is Bangkok; where the angels never sleep.

Around the Capital

Delicately carved ornamental decorations, like the one above, are as much a part of the Bangkok landscape as the *tuk-tuks* that speed by on the streets below them. This beguiling mixture of the sacred and the profane plays itself out in a variety of forms. Modernity and tradition, urban chaos and calm refinement – such dichotomies are unavoidable in the Great City of Angels.

Previous pages The gaudy *tuk-tuk* is as much part of Bangkok's transport scene as the yellow cab is in New York or the black taxi in London.

Above Wat Po covers 20 acres (9ha) to the south of the Grand Palace but many visitors arrive only to see the Reclining Buddha.

Right Thais are renown for their smiling faces – a childhood habit that just does not go away.

Opposite A view from the Shangri-La Hotel, with the Taksin Bridge – named after Bangkok's first military leader – spanning the Chao Phraya River.

Above A line of revellers following the tourists' haunt along the streets of Patpong is calmly observed by a Thai woman in traditional dress.

Below The availability of fast food in Bangkok does not depend on neon-lit, franchised restaurants (though there are plenty of these as well).

Left Every night of the year, stalls envelop the streets of Patpong and the pavements heave with visitors lured by the promise of counterfeit designer goods and bargain offers.

21

Above Detail of the temple wall at Wat Suthat, a superb temple in the old part of Bangkok that was begun in 1807 and not completed until 1851.

Above Bangkok's markets are astonishingly busy – a quarter of a million people visit Chatuchak every weekend – and yet market traders still find time to smile.

Above Canal transport, which has been an essential feature of Bangkok life from the 16th century, continues to serve a functional purpose in the traffic-strewn city.

Opposite At night, Wat Po illuminates these magnificent *chedi* (monuments built to house a Buddha relic), a word derived from Sanskrit that means memorial.

Above In a large gold shop like this one in Bangkok's Chinatown, where hallmarks can be trusted and quality assured as a rule, the problem is one of choice.

Right The gridlock that has made the city's traffic notorious has been relieved to some extent by the Skytrain system that passes overhead.

Left *Tuk-tuks* are not metered so fares are settled beforehand. While most drivers only speak Thai, they know how to negotiate in English.

Bangkok – Old and New

The history of Thailand is far older than the history of Bangkok but, since the late 18th century, the city at the mouth of the Chao Phraya River has established itself as the country's capital. At the dawn of the 21st century, Bangkok has an assured place as a premier metropolis of Southeast Asia, and for many savvy travellers it is a firm favourite, winning the accolade of being the region's most dynamic and multifaceted city.

Previous pages A line of contemplative Buddhas at Ayutthaya, only an hour from the capital by bus or three hours by a way of a leisurely cruise up the Chao Phraya River.

Opposite The Temple of Dawn, its Khmer-style tower over 80m (260ft) high, looks out across the Chao Phraya River.

Above A temple erected for the king's birthday. Reverence for the royal family is shared by virtually all Thais – everyone respects the playing of the national anthem at 8am each morning.

Below In portrayals of the Buddha there are four positions and postures that act as templates for the artist: sitting, walking, standing and reclining. A detail of the latter is shown here.

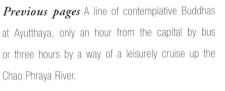

Right Although military parades continue the role of the military in Thai society has declined steadily over recent years.

Below A Skytrain weaves its way past the commercial district around Silom Road. By night, a multitude of popular eateries attract a less corporate crowd.

Left Photographs and mini-portraits of a past royal era take nostalgic pride of place in the front window of an antiquarian's shop.

Below The lure of consumerism beckons brightly amid the steel and glass of the Bis Mall, one of a host of modern shopping complexes in the capital.

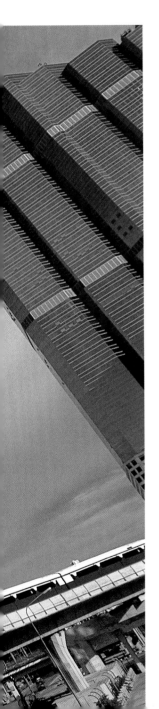

Above Wat Po, which houses the spectacular Reclining Buddha, is the largest temple-monastery in Bangkok and the oldest, dating back to the 16th century.

Opposite At Wat Phra Mahathat, Ayutthaya, a stone Buddha's placid head has found itself nestled none too coyly in the roots of a bodhi tree.

Above The Democracy Monument, a well-known city landmark in the Rattanakosin area of Bangkok where the principal royal buildings are located, was erected to commemorate Thailand's first constitution in 1932.

Opposite Bangkok's middle classes enjoy high-rise scenic views of the city from these modern condominium towers built in the 1980s.

Above Now in the heart of the old city, Vimarnmek Palace was built in 1901 as a royal retreat for King Chulalongkorn in what was then the suburbs of Bangkok.

Serenity and Enlightenment

Nearly 95 per cent of Thais subscribe to Buddhism, with Muslims making up the only significant religious minority. Buddhism, a philosophy as much as a religion, imbues most aspects of Thai life and helps account for the characteristic charm and ease with which Thais conduct themselves.

Previous Pages Carefully arranged garlands, donated as an offering by those who come to pray, are a familiar sight at Buddhist temples in Bangkok.

Above For these shaven-headed novices, monkhood not only gains spiritual merit for their families but also provides poor Thais with a means to continue their education beyond elementary level.

Left Captive birds, usually small finches, are sold so that the purchaser can release them and gain spiritual merit for such an act of compassion.

Opposite The most visited temple on the west side of the Chao Phraya River, Wat Arun (Temple of Dawn), is home to this golden Buddha, reputed to have been designed by Rama II.

Above Thailand's Muslim population, less than four per cent of the total population, mostly lives in the far south of the country near the border with Malaysia.

Above Thais with Chinese ancestry make up over 10 per cent of the population and their temples are mostly found in urban centres, especially Bangkok.

Left Thais make spiritual merit by lighting incense sticks and offering up a prayer at the Erawan Shrine, in the hope of improving their lot on the ladder of reincarnation.

Above It's written on this young woman's face – Buddhism's calm acceptance of the transitory nature of existence and the need to make the best of this life.

Left Historic murals on the walls of a monastery, testimony to the days before public education when a wat also served to disseminate knowledge about the Buddha's life.

Above Thais of Chinese ancestry have not forgotten their cultural heritage and they celebrate with their own festivals in Bangkok.

Top left A detail of artwork from Wat Phra Mahathat, Ayutthaya. Legend has it that a vision appearing to a 14th-century king led to the construction of the monastery.

Above This row of statues reflects a meditative mood in the *dhyana* posture, symbolized by both hands resting palms up on the Buddha's lap.

Opposite These young monks gazing at the Reclining Buddha, Wat Po, are no doubt transfixed by the dazzling 5m-wide (16ft) golden smile.

Above Hualampong Railway Station, Bangkok's main station, was built in the 1890s and followed the design of a Victorian main-line station from the north of England.

Right It is not unusual to find a small group of Thai men engrossed in a boardgame around a table on a street pavement or inside a coffee shop.

Above Thais, whether they are ethnic Thai, Chinese, Malay or Indian, share the same Thai national language, the medium of instruction in all schools.

Left A third-class railway carriage may not be ideal for a long-distance journey but it is more than adequate for a short, local trip.

Important Attractions

The extravagant detail and traditional forms of Thai architecture dominate the royal and religious buildings of Bangkok – the Grand Palace and many of the temples providing the best examples – and aspects of this style continue to influence modern designs. At the same time, the country has been open to aesthetic influences from abroad for many centuries and the resulting riot of architectural styles offers a visual treat for the visitor.

Previous pages The Grand Palace, deservedly the most visited sight in Bangkok, is as spectacular by day as it is by night.

Opposite Wat Po, the largest temple monastery in Bangkok and over 200 years old, boasts superb mother-of-pearl inlaid doors depicting episodes from the Hindu *Ramayana*.

Above Archaeological detail from Wat Phra Kaeo, home to Thailand's most important religious image, the Emerald Buddha, and visited daily by both Thai pilgrims and tourists.

Right A ferocious-looking *singha* – a mythical guardian lion – made of bronze stands guard outside a wat to ward off evil.

Above The Grand Palace complex covers an area of over 1.5km² (1 sq mile), including these serene gardens that offer a refuge from the constant flood of visitors.

Right The architectural plan of Ayutthaya was copied exactly in the building of the Grand Palace, including the employment of the country's most skilled goldsmiths.

Above Murals depicting episodes from the Ramakien, a Thai version of the Hindu *Ramayana*, in the cloisters surrounding Wat Phra Kaeo.

Left The Ramakien murals, consisting of 178 panels, were first painted during the reign of Rama in the late 18th century but they have been restored a number of times.

Top left Wat Saket, *saket* meaning washing of hair, derives its name from the fact that Rama I stopped here to bathe on returning from Laos with the Emerald Buddha.

Top right Mother-of-pearl inlay work on one of the feet of the Reclining Buddha, Wat Po.

Far left In the urban epicenter of modern Bangkok, Jim Thompson's house and its contents faithfully recreate traditional Thai forms.

Left Elephants and an armed guard stand to attention outside the Grand Palace.

Opposite The smiling face of the dying Reclining Buddha, about to enter the state of nirvana.

Above Bangkok's Chinatown has been home to Chinese immigrants since the 1780s; today, most Thais of Chinese descent are second or third-generation Cantonese or Hainanese.

Left Shrines are ubiquitous in Bangkok and may be seen in a restaurant, a hotel lobby or, as shown here, in a busy clothing market.

Above Thais of Chinese descent practise Mahayana Buddhism, making more use of candles, incense and lucky charms than the mainstream Theravada Buddhism.

Above The third and fourth floors of the River City Shopping Centre are packed with high quality art and craft shops offering quality merchandise from all parts of the country.

Above T-shirts counterfeiting famous brand names and their logos are a favourite purchase with tourists, chiefly due to the very low prices.

Above The Siam Discovery Centre might sound like some hands-on science museum but it is in fact an upmarket shopping mall selling pricey designer goods.

Opposite The MBK Centre, a vast shopping mall packed to the steel rafters with clothes, electronics and much more, is where locals and discerning tourists shop.

Above A tourist ghetto of sorts, but no self-respecting budget backpacker would stay anywhere else other than in or around Khao San Road.

Left Street stalls like this one on Khao San Road display their wares, seven days a week, from 10 in the morning right through until 10 at night.

Below On the Khao San Road, travellers don't need to look far to satisfy their needs: transport, accommodation, foreign exchange, food and drink and much more.

Exploring the Colourful Markets

Long after the T-shirts have faded and the counterfeit watches are dismantled, the merchandise that lasts comes from the skilled hands of Thai artisans. The long-standing tradition of arts and crafts, once nurtured by the court and temples, flourishes as never before and the visitor is spoilt for choice in gold and silver jewellery, wood carvings, ornaments, delicate pewter work and silks.

Previous Pages A group of little dancers awaits its cue to appear in the central arena of the Rose Garden, near Bangkok, where regular tourist shows are held.

Above Available in Bangkok, the best quality metalwork, like this silverwork from Chiang Mai, is produced by silversmiths from the north of the country.

Left Music is an essential component of Thai theatre and a xylophone-like instrument is a familiar part of a classical orchestra.

Opposite Thai dance is inseparable from drama and subtle movements of the hands and body express fine degrees of emotion.

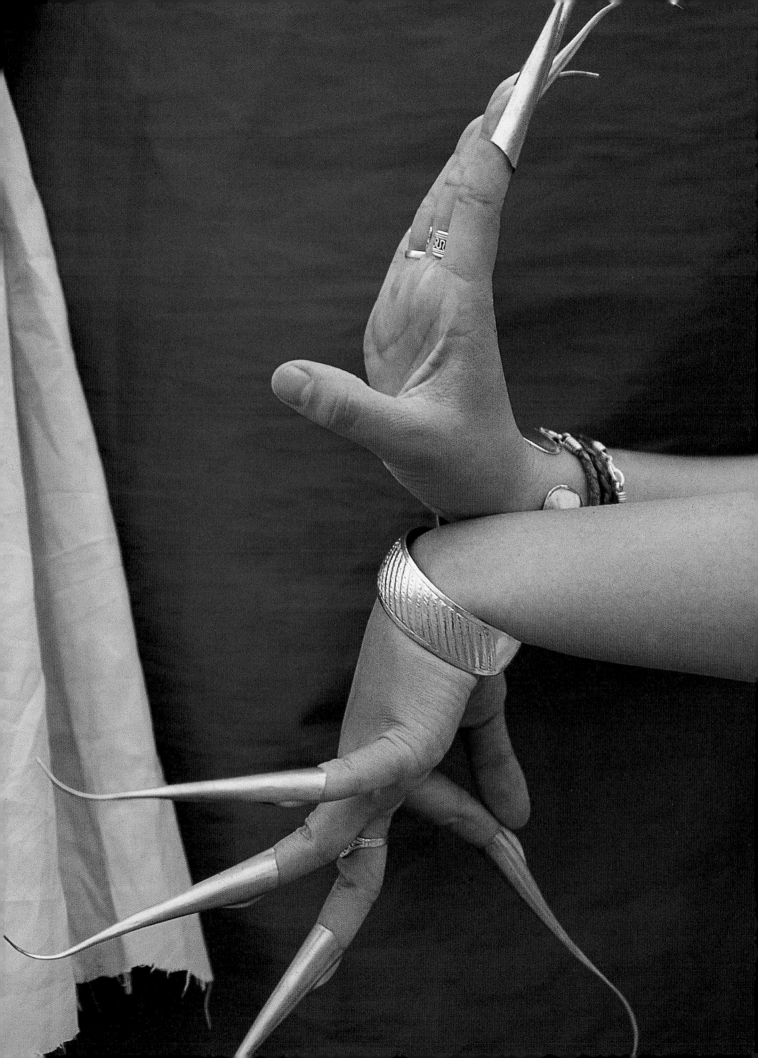

Above The finished products from this silk-weaving factory in Chiang Mai are likely to end up with one of Bangkok's many tailors.

Above Thicker than European and Chinese silks and ideal for dyeing, finished Thai silk can be tailored into smart suits, ties, dresses and much else besides.

Left Puppet dolls dressed in hilltribe and classical dance costumes are readily available in Bangkok, along with embroidery work and wooden carvings.

Above A form of folk art to some, baskets of all shapes and sizes are sold in local markets for their functional value.

Left The restoration and maintenance of ancient artwork, as shown here in the Grand Palace, is an on-going process.

Above Traditional Thai dances are performed in a variety of venues in Bangkok, from restaurants to theatres.

Above The lilting and airy sounds of Thai music lighten the mood at one of Bangkok's night markets.

Above These silken-clad, traditional Thai dancers could be mistaken for partici-pants in a beauty pageant as they take up positions for their performance.

Opposite The kicking blows in Thai boxing have a visual impact for the audience, but the really effective strikes are delivered with the knee or elbow.

Above Performances of shadow puppet plays, mentioned in Buddhist literature over two millennia ago, are becoming increasingly rare in the age of electronic entertainment.

Right The art of making shadow puppets is thought to have originated in India and spread to Thailand via Java.

Above One of Thailand's ancient crafts, woodcarving is time-consuming work – a quality product such as this one may take months to complete.

Left Delicacy and finesse are characteristic features of Thai crafts, shown here by decorative wood and pewter containers showcasing bars of carved soap.

The Taste of Bangkok

Hygiene-conscious visitors to Bangkok tend to shy away from roadside food stalls but in so doing risk missing out on a wealth of local dishes. Cooked in minutes, often in full view of customers and using market fresh produce, Bangkok's fast food is as delicious to eat as it is inexpensive to buy. Those interested in a more formal setting can sample superb dishes presented with flair at a number of Bangkok's top restaurants.

Previous pages Thai food is an aromatic adventure of exotic flavours and exciting textures. The fragrant curries are simply irresistible.

Opposite This display at a fruit and vegetable stall at the Chatuchak weekend market includes popular papayas, hanging on the left, and bright red rambutans at the front.

Above Like *nouvelle cuisine* in the West, the aesthetic appeal of food presentation – as in this carved fruit – is of extreme importance in Thai cuisine.

Right As a general rule, the smaller and more innocuous looking the chilli, the fiercer the heat!

Above Typical variety of a Thai shared meal. The bowl in the middle contains *tom yam* soup, a broth made with lemon grass and coconut milk that can be extremely hot if cooked with whole chillies.

Right The wok is a fundamental piece of equipment in Thai stir-fried cooking, allowing the entire surface to heat up while retaining extra heat in the centre.

Above A typical Bangkok food stall, filled to the brim with a mouthwatering display of noodle dishes, fried rice, and several varieties of curries and seafoods – all freshly cooked.

Left Kitchens on carts set up their fast-food stalls in designated night-market areas or pop up impromptu wherever there may be customers.

Above What you see is what you get — sausages on skewers are cooked on the street using a mobile gas burner.

Above Thailand's most famous beer is Singha, acrid-tasting to some palates but also available in a lighter version called Singha Gold.

Above The idea of solitary eating can be anathema to many Thais, the enjoyment of food being a characteristically social event.

Opposite A seemingly bewildering array of small dried fish — a popular ingredient in many local dishes — are sold daily at Bangkok's dry fish market.

Right A small selection of *gaeng* (curry) dishes, many based on coconut milk and ranging from bland and mild to the fiery and unquenchably hot.

Above A local Thai woman and her cat wait patiently for a customer at a Bangkok market. It is not uncommon to see elderly women manning stalls.

Right Vendors arrange their produce at Damnoen Saduak, a town some 100km (60 miles) from Bangkok, famous for its floating market.

Copyright rests with the following photographers and/or their agents. Key to Locations: t = top; tl = top left; tc = top centre; tr = top right; b = bottom; bl = bottom left; bc = bottom centre; br = bottom right; l = left; r = right; c = centre; cl = centre left; cr = centre right. (No abbreviation is given for pages with a single image, or pages on which all photographs are by same photographer.)

AB	Adrian Baker	**GZC**	Geraldine Z Cupido	**JS**	Jeroen Snijders
ABL	Anders Blomqvist	**GITS**	Gallo Images/Tony Stone	**MA**	Mark Azavedo
AH	Allan Hartley	**HL**	Hutchison Library	**MO**	Mikihiko Ohta
APL	Axiom Photo Library	**JB**	Jeanette Baker	**MW**	Mark Williams
CC	Chris Caldicott	**JH**	Jeremy Horner	**NS**	Neil Setchfield
GC	Gerald Cubitt	**JIH**	Jim Holmes	**NSU**	Nicholas Sumner

PB	Peter Baker	**RF**	Robert Francis
PBB	Big Pie Pictures	**RS**	Robin Smith
PBK	Photobank	**SC**	Sylvia Cordaiy
PC	Paul Chesley	**TI**	Travel Ink
PF	Patrick Ford	**TSE**	The Seeing Eye
PT	Pauline Thornton	**VM**	Valerie Martin

Page	Pos	Credit	Page	Pos	Credit	Page	Pos	Credit	Page	Pos	Credit
1		GZC	21	t	APL/JIH	42	tr	NS	62	b	PBK/PB
2	t	PBK/PB	21	b	SC	42	b	TSE/ABL	63		JS
2	b	PBK/AB	22	tl	TSE/ABL	43		JS	64		HL
3	l	GC	22	tr	PBK/PB	44	t	TSE/ABL	65	t	GC
3	r	PBK/AB	22	b	PBK/AB	44	b	NS	65	cl	GC
4		TI/PF	23		TSE/ABL	45	t & b	JS	65	cr	JS
5	t	GC	24	t	GC	46-47		GC	65	b	JS
5	b	GZC	24	b	JS	48		APL/CC	66	tl	RS
6	l	TI/AH	25	b	NS	49	t	GC	66	tr	PBK/PB
6	r	TI/PT	26-27		VM	49	b	GZC	66	b	PBK/PB
7	l	NS	28		PBK/AB	50	t	GC	67		PBK/PB
7	r	PBK/JB	29	t	JS	50	b	PBK/AB	68	t	JS
8	t	VM	29	b	SC	51	t	APL/MO	68	bl	JS
8	b	TSE/ABL	30	b	HL/JH	51	b	JS	68	br	JS
9		TSE/ABL	30	t	JS	52	tl	JS	69	t	RS
10	t	MA	31	t & b	JS	52	tr	GC	69	b	SC
10	b	HL/JH	32		GZC	52	bl	GC	70-71		NS
11	l&r	PBK/PB	33		TSE/ABL	52	br	JS	72		GC
12	t	GC	34		PBK/PB	53		PBK/PB	73	t	JS
12	b	SC	35	t	HL/RF	54		JS	73	b	VM
13	l	VM	35	b	TSE/ABL	55	t	NS	74	t	VM
13	r	GC	36-37		MA	55	b	GITS/MW	74	b	PBK/PB
14	t	JS	38	t	JS	56	tl	GC	75	t	GC
14	b	VM	38	b	NS	56	tr	NS	75	b	NS
15	l	VM	39		TI	56	b	NS	76	t	APL/JIH
15	r	PBK/PB	40		SC	57		MA	76	bl & br	NS
16-17		HL/JH	41	t	JS	58		SC	77		PBK/PB
18	t	TSE/ABL	41	cl	JS	59	t	HL/JH	78	t	VM
18	b	PBK/JB	41	cr	PBK/PB	59	b	NS	78	b	PBK/PB
19		GC	41	b	GC	60-61		GITS/PC	79		RS
20		HL/JH	42	tl	GZC	62	t	JS			

ASIA BOOKS

Published and Distributed by
Asia Books Co., Ltd.
5 Sukhumvit Road Soi 61,
P.O. Box 40,
Bangkok 10110, Thailand
Tel: (66 2) 715-9000 ext. 3202 – 4
Fax: (66 2) 714-2799
E-mail: information@asiabooks.com
www.asiabooks.com

ISBN 1 84330 117 2

Publisher Mariëlle Renssen
Publishing Manager Claudia Dos Santos,
Managing Editor Simon Pooley
Editor Ingrid Corbett
Designer Geraldine Cupido
Picture researcher Colleen Abrahams
Production Myrna Collins
Cartographer Carl Germishuys

Reproduction by Hirt & Carter (Cape) Pty Ltd
Printed and bound in Malaysia by
Times Offset (M) Sdn. Bhd.

10 9 8 7 6 5 4 3 2 1